D0941084

DOCTOR STRANGE VOL. 4: MR. MISERY PREMIERE. Contains material
originally published in magazine form as DOCTOR STRANGE #17-20 and
ANNUAL #1. First printing 2017. ISBN# 978-1-302-90586-6. Published by MARVEL
WORLDWIDE, INC., a subsidiary of MARVEL ENTERTAINMENT, LLC. OFFICE OF PUB-
LICATION: 135 West 50th Street, New York, NY 10020. Copyright © 2017 MARVEL No
similarity between any of the names, characters, persons, and/or institutions in this magazine
with those of any living or dead person or institution is intended, and any such similarity which may
exist is purely coincidental. **Printed in the U.S.A.** DAN BUCKLEY, President, Marvel Entertainment; JOE
QUESADA, Chief Creative Officer; TOM BREVOORT, SVP of Publishing; DAVID BOGART, SVP of Business Affairs &
Operations, Publishing & Partnership; C.B. CEBULSKI, VP of Brand Management & Development, Asia; DAVID GABRIEL,
SVP of Sales & Marketing, Publishing; JEFF YOUNGQUIST, VP of Production & Special Projects; DAN CARR, Executive Director
of Publishing Technology; ALEX MORALES, Director of Publishing Operations; SUSAN CRESPI, Production Manager; STAN LEE,
Chairman Emeritus. For information regarding advertising in Marvel Comics or on Marvel.com, please contact Vit DeBellis, Integrated
Sales Manager, at vdebellis@marvel.com. For Marvel subscription inquiries, please call 888-511-5480. **Manufactured between 7/28/2017
and 8/29/2017 by LSC COMMUNICATIONS INC., KENDALLVILLE, IN, USA.**

10 9 8 7 6 5 4 3 2 1

DOCTOR STRANGE CREATED BY
STAN LEE & STEVE DITKO

COLLECTION EDITOR: **JENNIFER GRÜNWALD**
ASSISTANT EDITOR: **CAITLIN O'CONNELL**
ASSOCIATE MANAGING EDITOR: **KATERI WOODY**
EDITOR, SPECIAL PROJECTS: **MARK D. BEAZLEY**
VP, PRODUCTION & SPECIAL PROJECTS: **JEFF YOUNGQUIST**
SVP PRINT, SALES & MARKETING: **DAVID GABRIEL**
BOOK DESIGNER: **JAY BOWEN**

EDITOR IN CHIEF: **AXEL ALONSO**
CHIEF CREATIVE OFFICER: **JOE QUESADA**
PRESIDENT: **DAN BUCKLEY**
EXECUTIVE PRODUCER: **ALAN FINE**

DOCTOR STRANGE

Mr. Misery

ISSUE #17

Jason Aaron
WRITER

Frazer Irving
ARTIST

Kevin Nowlan
COVER ART

ISSUES #18-19

Jason Aaron
WRITER

Chris Bachalo
PENCILER/COLORIST

Al Vey, Tim Townsend, John Livesay, Victor Olazaba, Jamie Mendoza & Wayne Faucher
INKERS

Patrick Brown (#18)
& Kevin Nowlan (#19)
COVER ART

ISSUE #20

Jason Aaron
WRITER

Chris Bachalo & Kevin Nowlan
ARTISTS/COLORISTS

Al Vey, John Livesay, Tim Townsend, Jaime Mendoza, Victor Olazaba & Kevin Nowlan
INKERS

Chris Bachalo & Tim Townsend
COVER ART

ANNUAL #1

"TO GET HER. FOREVER."

KATHRYN IMMONEN
WRITER

LEONARDO ROMERO
ARTIST

JORDIE BELLAIRE
COLORIST

"STRANGE TALES: YAO, THE NOT-QUITE-ANCIENT ONE"

ROBBIE THOMPSON
WRITER

JONATHAN MARKS
ARTIST

LEE LOUGHRIDGE
COLORS

W. SCOTT FORBES
COVER ART

VC's Cory Petit
LETTERER

Allison Stock
ASSISTANT EDITOR

Darren Shan
ASSOCIATE EDITOR

Nick Lowe
EDITOR

IT SEEMS LIKE JUST THE OTHER DAY WHEN ALL THE MAGIC DISAPPEARED.

DO. DIE-DIE.

A SCIENCE CULT CALLED THE *EMPIRIKUL* KILLED IT.

DO. DIE-DIE DO.

PEOPLE SUFFERED. PEOPLE DIED. BUT WE STOPPED THE BAD GUYS.

AND SINCE THEN, MAGIC HAS SLOWLY BEEN RETURNING.

DIE-DIE-DIE!

DIE-DIE!

MAGICAL FLORA AND FAUNA HAVE BEEN SPAWNING AND FLOWERING AGAIN. THE DRAGON LINES THROUGHOUT THE EARTH ARE ONCE AGAIN HUMMING WITH POWER.

AND WITH THOSE ENERGIES, COME THE STRANGE AND WONDERFUL CREATURES THAT FEED ON THEM.

WHICH BRINGS US TO TODAY.

HEY!

UM, IS THERE AN ALERT IN THERE ABOUT YOUR *KITCHEN*? BECAUSE I WAS ALMOST KILLED WALKING PAST IT TODAY.

NOT SURE IF WONG LEFT THE FRIDGE OPEN OR WHAT, BUT THERE WERE TENTACLES THE SIZE OF CROCODILES COMING OUT OF THE DOOR.

DON'T GO IN THE KITCHEN WITHOUT A FLAMETHROWER, ZELMA. OR BETTER YET, JUST ORDER TAKEOUT.

WONG IS THE ONLY ONE WHO KNOWS HOW TO KEEP THIS HOUSE FROM KILLING US *ALL*, ISN'T HE?

ANY MORE PROBLEMS IN THE SANCTUM WILL HAVE TO WAIT. OR IN THE *REST* OF THE WORLD, FOR THAT MATTER. WONG IS THE PRIORITY HERE.

STAY ON THE PHONE, ZELMA, UNTIL YOU'VE TALKED TO EVERY LAST CAPTAIN AMERICA, WOLVERINE, AND IRON-PERSON.

IF HE'S NOT KIDNAPPED, DOC...THEN WHAT *IS* HE?

IF I'M RIGHT... VISHANTI BE WITH HIM...

"...HE'S WISHING HE WAS *DEAD*."

TELL ME HOW TO *HURT* THE DOCTOR.

OH STEPHEN. STEPHEN, FORGIVE ME, I CANNOT...

HEH.

YES. OH YES, I *SEE*. THAT WILL DO QUITE NICELY.

WELL DONE, WONG.

WE'D BETTER GET GOING, THEN. WE'VE GOT A LOT OF WORK TO DO, DON'T WE?

OR *UNDO*, I SHOULD SAY. HEH.

THE BAR WITH NO DOORS.

"NICE *WHEELS*, DOC! AND I IMAGINE IT'S LESS TAXING THAN A FLIGHT SPELL."

BUT, I MUST SAY, YOU NEVER STRUCK ME AS A HARLEY KINDA GUY.

IF I LIKED TO DRIVE THINGS THAT WENT SLOW, I'D STILL BE LIVING ON THE UPPER EAST SIDE AND CUTTING INTO PEOPLE'S BRAINS FOR $1,000 AN HOUR.

INSTEAD, I'M *HERE*. PLEASE TELL THIS WAS WORTH MY TIME.

WISH WE COULD, DOC. BUT NONE OF US HAVE HEARD SO MUCH AS A MYSTICAL PEEP ON THE STREETS.

NOTHING ABOUT WONG OR THIS MR. MISERY GUY.

AND, IN CASE YOU HAVEN'T NOTICED, BUSINESS IS REALLY PICKING UP OUT THERE THESE DAYS. FOR *ALL* OF US.

IN SIBERIA, IT RAIN DEAD BIRDS. THEN BIRDS COME BACK AS *ZOMBIES*. EAT BEAR. *COUNT KAOZ* HERE MISSING ALL THE FUN.

OF COURSE WE WANT TO HELP, STEPHEN. BUT YOU'RE GONNA HAVE TO FILL US IN A BIT MORE.

YOU'VE NEVER REALLY TOLD US WHO THIS MR. MISERY GUY *IS*, OR EXACTLY WHERE IT WAS HE CAME FROM.

WE ALWAYS TALK ABOUT HOW IMPORTANT IT IS TO PAY THE TAB WHEN YOU DO WHAT WE DO FOR A LIVING.

MISERY IS WHAT HAPPENS WHEN YOU DON'T PAY IT THE *RIGHT* WAY.

MORE THAN ANYTHING, HE WANTS TO SEE ME *SUFFER.* WHICH IS WHY I HAVE TO FIND WONG, AS SOON AS POSSIBLE.

AGAMOTTO KNOWS WHAT THAT BASTARD WILL DO TO HIM IF I DON'T...

WHAT THE... WE'RE UNDER ATTACK?!

NO, I DON'T THINK SO.

ARE YOU KIDDING ME? LOOK AT MY FLOOR! I JUST GOT THIS PLACE PUT BACK TOGETHER.

THIS BAR IS SUPPOSED TO BE FOR SORCERERS ONLY. SO, ALRIGHT, FESS UP...

...WHICH OF YOU JERKS INVITED THE **MAN-THING?**

I THINK HE'S HERE FOR ME, BUT I DON'T HAVE TIME FOR WHATEVER HE'S--

HSSSS

GAAGGH!

DON'T SAY IT. NOBODY BETTER SAY...

EL QUE CONOCE MIEDO, QUEMA AL TOQUE DE MAN-THING.

I SAID DON'T SAY IT!

YES, I'M AFRAID! I COULD'VE JUST **TOLD** YOU THAT! YOU DIDN'T HAVE TO...

I THINK YOU'D BETTER GO WITH HIM, STEPHEN, OR YOU'RE LOOKING AT A **HUG** YOU WON'T SOON FORGET.

THIS HAD BETTER BE GOOD, MR. GREEN JEANS.

KNOCK
KNOCK

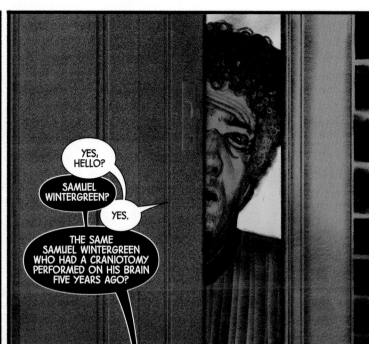

YES, HELLO?

SAMUEL WINTERGREEN?

YES.

THE SAME SAMUEL WINTERGREEN WHO HAD A CRANIOTOMY PERFORMED ON HIS BRAIN FIVE YEARS AGO?

DO I KNOW YOU? WHAT IS THIS?

IT WOULD APPEAR YOUR SURGERY WAS A SUCCESS, SAMUEL. THOUGH I'M AFRAID I'VE GOT SOME VERY BAD NEWS FOR YOU.

THAT *TUMOR* THE DOCTOR REMOVED...

...IT LOOKS TO ME LIKE IT'S *COMING BACK.*

...IT FOUGHT BACK.

VISHANTI BE WITH HIM.

BY THAT POINT, WE'D, UH... WE'D DISCOVERED THERE WAS A *CONNECTION* BETWEEN THE PATIENTS.

THEY'D ALL HAD BRAIN SURGERY BEFORE. SUCCESSFULLY. SOME YEARS AGO.

AND IN EACH OF THEIR CASES... THEIR SURGERIES WERE PERFORMED BY *YOU.*

LET ME SEE THEM. *NOW.*

SAMUEL WINTERGREEN. I REMEMBER HIM. ONE OF MY LAST PATIENTS BEFORE...

DOCTOR STRANGE, WHAT *IS* THIS? WHAT'S HAPPENED TO THESE PEOPLE?

MISERY.

MISERY HAS HAPPENED.

HAVE THEM PREPPED FOR SURGERY.

BUT...YOU SAW WHAT HAPPENED TO THE *LAST* SURGEON. WHATEVER IS...INSIDE THEM, OUR ANESTHESIA HAS NO EFFECT.

I'VE GOT A POCKET FULL OF ALGAE THAT I EXPECT MIGHT BE OF USE, ONCE WE'VE EXTRACTED THE NEOSAXITOXIN FROM IT.

I SAVED THESE PEOPLE ONCE. I CAN DO IT AGAIN.

PREP THEM. *ALL* OF THEM. THEN CLEAR THE HOSPITAL. THE ENTIRE BLOCK, IF YOU CAN.

BUT NOT WITHOUT SOME QUALIFIED ASSISTANCE.

I TOOK THE LIBERTY OF MAKING A CALL.

KRAKA-KOOM

THE WORLD'S FINEST
SUPER-SURGEONS

YOU'RE STALLING, STEPHEN.

THIS IS NOT THE FIGHT, AND YOU KNOW IT.

YOU'RE STALLING BECAUSE YOU KNOW YOU CAN'T WIN. BUT BY ALL MEANS, DO GO AHEAD AND TRY.

I'LL BE WATCHING.

WHERE'S *WONG*, YOU BASTARD? WHERE'S...

TCHAK

THE BEAST HAS FLED. BUT THE HUM OF MJOLNIR IN MY HAND TELLS ME THE DANGER HAS NOT YET PASSED.

NOT IN THE LEAST.

THE HOSPITAL HAS BEEN CLEARED OF EVERYONE EXCEPT THOSE ALREADY INFECTED.

HOW WILL WE SAVE THEM FROM THAT SHADOW BEAST?

THE SAME WAY I SAVED THEM BEFORE.

ONE INCISION AT A TIME.

C'MON, THOR. WE'RE WANTED IN *SURGERY.*

WHAT THE HELL IS *THIS?*

GAGGH, I CAN'T EAT THIS CRAP!

SMELLS LIKE HOT GARBAGE! BOILED IN OTHER, HOTTER GARBAGE!

I JUST CLIMBED A STUPID MOUNTAIN IN TIBET WITH TWO RUINED HANDS! I NEED *REAL* FOOD!

SOMEBODY GET ME A STEAK! I DON'T CARE IF IT COMES OFF A *YAK,* BUT I DEMAND A--

THERE IS NO STEAK HERE.

NO RED MEAT AT ALL.

THERE ARE ALSO NO *DEMANDS.*

WHAT? WHO THE CRAP ARE *YOU?*

I AM THE ONE WHO MADE THIS..."HOT GARBAGE," A YOU CALL IT.

I AM A DISCIPLE OF ANCIENT ON JUST AS YO WISH TO B

YOU CAN'T WIN THIS. WE BOTH KNOW IT.

I'VE DONE MORE EXORCISMS THAN YOU'VE GOT EYEBALLS, MISERY. AND THEY ALWAYS END THE SAME WAY.

IT'S AN EXORCISM FOR *YOU,* DOCTOR. FOR ME IT'S A VERY DIFFERENT SORT OF PROCEDURE.

AN *AUTOPSY.*

POOR LITTLE WONG...WOULD YOU LIKE TO KNOW HOW YOUR FRIEND *DIED?*

BY THE LIGHT OF THE VISHANTI, I COMMAND YOU--

I'M NOT SOME DEMON OF THE NETHERWORLD.

YOUR SPELLS DON'T WORK ON ME.

YOU'RE *LYING!* I KNOW HE'S NOT DEAD!

AH YES, YOU KNOW *EVERYTHING* ABOUT YOUR DEAR FRIEND WONG, DON'T YOU? TELL ME...

WHAT IS WONG'S FAVORITE *FOOD?*

HE'S EATEN IT EVERY MORNING FOR BREAKFAST SINCE HE WAS FIVE.

WHAT IS IT?

WE'RE NOT HERE TO TALK ABOUT FOOD.

HA HA HA HA HA H H

BY THE LIGHT OF THE VISHANTI AND THE POWER OF THE DWELLERS IN DARKNESS--

I'VE RUMMAGED THROUGH THE RECESSES OF WONG'S MEMORIES, LOOKING FOR THE SHARPEST DAGGER WITH WHICH TO STAB YOU. AND I *FOUND* IT.

BY THE SEVEN RINGS OF RAGGADORR--

THE THREE MOST HURTFUL WORDS A PERSON CAN EVER HEAR.

I LOVE YOU.

YOU BASTARD. DON'T YOU DO THIS.

WONG LOVES YOU. LIKE A FATHER LOVES HIS SON. HE'S DEVOTED HIS ENTIRE LIFE TO YOU.

HE HAS NO WIFE, NO FAMILY. NO LIFE BEYOND THIS SANCTUM.

WHEN HE DIES, HIS FAMILY LINE DIES WITH HIM.

YET STILL HE LOVES YOU. WITH ALL HIS BEING.

AND YOU CAN'T RETURN THE FAVOR, CAN YOU?

DAMN IT, IN THE NAME OF THE ALL-SEEING AGAMOTTO!

RRRRGGHHH!!

HAHAHAAAHA

*

HA HA HAAA.

I'VE BEEN GOING ABOUT THIS ALL WRONG.

BUT SO HAVE YOU.

LOVE. THAT'S HOW YOU THINK YOU CAN *HURT* ME?

LOVE'S NOT EVEN IN THE JOB DESCRIPTION FOR A SORCERER SUPREME.

BUT YOU KNOW WHAT IS?

PAIN.

GGRRRRRRGGGGHH!!!

WHAT... WHAT ARE YOU DOING...

YOU REMEMBER MY PAIN, DON'T YOU, OLD BUDDY? YOU SHOULD. IT'S WHAT YOU'RE *MADE* OF.

AND YOU WANT IT *AGAIN,* DON'T YOU?

STOP THAT.

YOU'RE DRAWN TO IT.

NO... YOU...

DOCTOR STRANGE? STEPHEN, IS THAT YOU?

WONG? DON'T...

HHRRRRRGGGH!!!

BY THE LIGHT OF THE...

GAAGGGH!!!

YEARS AGO.

ARE YOU SURE THIS IS A GOOD IDEA?

UH. NO?

NO, NOT *REALLY*, I GUESS. NOT AT ALL.

I'M NOT SURE *ANYTHING* I'VE BEEN DOING FOR MONTHS NOW HAS BEEN WHAT YOU COULD CALL "A GOOD IDEA," WONG...

RUN, ZELMA!

MISERY IS IN THE SANCTUM! YOUR HOUSE IS *POSSESSED!*

GAGGH, WHO'S THE IDIOT WHO PLANTED ALL THESE TREES?!

WE'VE GOT TO GET TO THE FRONT DOOR! GOT TO GET WONG OUT...

WE'RE ALMOST TO THE...

GUUGH!

UH, DOC.

THIS IS *REALLY* NOT A GOOD TIME TO GET KNOCKED OUT. YOU DO REALIZE WE'RE RIGHT OUTSIDE THE...

...KITCHEN. OF COURSE IT HAD TO BE THE DAMN KITCHEN.

ONLY ONE WAY OUT OF THIS, ISN'T THERE? GOTTA FIND SOMETHING TO HELP WAKE UP THE DOC. THAT MEANS...

SORRY, FRYING PAN, GUESS I GOTTA SEE A MAN ABOUT A FIRE.

YOU GUYS JUST GO AHEAD AND LIE THERE FOR A SECOND.

LUNCH IS ON ME.

WE WAKE UP WONG.

I'M ALL OUT OF BULLETS AND ...ES, DOC. WHAT ...DO WE DO?

I NEED YOU TO WAKE UP *NOW*, WONG. I NEED YOU TO HEAR WHAT I'M ABOUT TO SAY.

WONG! LISTEN TO ME! MISERY...

...MISERY WAS *RIGHT!*

I *DON'T* LOVE YOU! I *DON'T* LOVE *ANYONE!*

I CAN'T! I CAN'T CARE ABOUT PEOPLE BECAUSE...

...BECAUSE THEY'RE JUST *THINGS* TO ME! THEY HAVE TO BE! SACKS OF MEAT WITH SOULS INSIDE!

LOVE IS FOR CHILDREN AND POETS AND FOOLS!

DOC, WHAT THE HELL ARE YOU SAYING? GARRGH, DOC...!

WONG, I NEED YOU TO HEAR ME NOW!

WONG! I DON'T LOVE YOU! AND I NEVER WILL!

WONG, ARE YOU...

I'M STARVING.

WHAT'S FOR BREAKFAST?

I HAVE NO IDEA. STEPHEN SAID HE WOULD BE PROCURING SOMETHING.

HE'S FORBIDDEN ME FROM COOKING UNTIL HE'S SATISFIED I'VE RECOVERED FROM MY ORDEAL.

AND BESIDES, IT APPEARS SOMEONE VICIOUSLY GUNNED DOWN MY REFRIGERATOR.

YEAH, DON'T BLAME ME. THAT THING TOTALLY HAD IT COMING.

WHERE IS THE DOC, ANYWAY?

BLARRRGGGH!

WHO'S HUNGRY FOR BREAKFAST?

I'VE GOT PIZZA BAGELS WITH A SIDE OF BREAKFAST TACOS FOR ZELMA.

ALL MY FAVORITE FOOD GROUPS IN ONE!

AND FOR WONG, YOUR FAVORITE FOOD...

...OATMEAL WITH RAISINS.

SMELLS DELIGHTFUL, STEPHEN.

BUT I THOUGHT YOUR FAVORITE FOOD WAS--

HUSH.

STEPHEN... ARE YOU SURE YOU'RE ALL RIGHT?

NEVER... NEVER FELT BETTER. I JUST...

WONG, I WANT YOU TO KNOW...EVERYTHING I SAID TO YOU, WHEN MISERY WAS...

YOU DON'T HAVE TO EXPLAIN, STEPHEN.

I KNOW THAT WHAT YOU SAID WAS ONLY MEANT TO CAUSE YOU PAIN. SO MISERY WOULD BE DRAWN TO YOU, *REABSORBED* BY YOU.

I DIDN'T BELIEVE IT, STEPHEN. NOT FOR A MOMENT.

MISERY WAS THE MONSTER. NOT *YOU*.

RIGHT.

SO HOW DO WE REPLACE THE FRIDGE? IS THERE A SORCERER'S GROCERY STORE ANYWHERE AROUND HERE? MAYBE IN GREENPOINT?

FOR STARTERS, WE'LL HAVE TO MAKE A TRIP TO THE DARK DIMENSION.

WHY? TO FIGHT DORMAMMU?

NO. TO GO FISHING.

HA.

I LOVE YOU, DOCTOR STRANGE.

DOC? DOC, WHERE ARE YOU...

BLAAAAUUURGGH!

SOLD! TO THE GOAT IN THE BACK FOR THREE PHOENIX FEATHERS!

...I GIVE YOU THE FABLED *WAND OF XYGGONDO.* ONCE WIELDED BY RASPUTIN HIMSELF.

IN THE WAKE OF THE VICIOUS PURGE BY THE SCIENCE CULTISTS OF THE *EMPIRIKUL,* THIS IS ONE OF THE FEW MAGICAL ITEMS STILL LEFT ACTIVE AND EMPOWERED ON THIS PLANE OF EXISTENCE.

LET THE BIDDING COMMENCE.

CONGRATULATIONS, SIR GOAT. YOU AND YOUR MASTER ARE NOW THE PROUD OWNERS OF A GENUINE *HIMALAYAN YETI.* YOU MAY COLLECT HIM AT THE DOOR AS YOU LEAVE.

AND AS ALWAYS, WE THANK YOU FAMILIARS AND ACOLYTES, AS WELL AS YOUR VARIOUS MAGISTERS AND MISTRESSES, FOR YOUR PATRONAGE HERE AT THE *HOUSE OF THE INFERNAL GLORIES.*

NEXT UP... OH, *THIS* IS THE ITEM YOU'VE ALL BEEN WAITING FOR...

RECENTLY RECOVERED FROM THE WELL OF THE RISING PESTILENCE IN STONIA, AND VERIFIED BY OUR MYSTICAL APPRAISERS...

I BID NINE BARRELS OF RAT BLOOD!

THREE HUNDRED FROG HEARTS!

A DOZEN CANDLES OF HUMAN TALLOW AND THE TEARS OF THE WORLD'S OLDEST VIRGIN!

I BID THE SOUL OF MY MOTHER!

I BID ALL OF YOUR TEETH!

I BID ONE MILLION GOAT HORNS FOR THE RIGHT TO MURDER DR. STRANGE!

I BID TWO MILLION CROW EYES!

JUST KILL THE BASTARD!

SORRY. HATE TO KISS AND RUN.

USED TO BE, THE WORLD WAS PRACTICALLY *LITTERED* WITH MAGICAL WEAPONS LIKE THIS WAND. NOW, THERE ARE BARELY ANY LEFT.

AND USED TO BE, IF I WANTED TO DROP INTO A PLACE LIKE THIS TO KEEP POWER FROM FALLING INTO THE WRONG HANDS, ALL I HAD TO DO WAS WIGGLE MY FINGERS AND I'D BE IN AND OUT IN A *FLASH*.

KRSSH

THOSE SURE WERE GRAND OLD DAYS.

THACK

ARRGGH!

DOC!

IN THE NAME OF THE WITCH QUEEN *MORGAN LE FAY*, HAND OVER THE WAND OR DIE IN THESE SKIES!

MAGMA MAN. FEEL LIKE HE...SHOT ME WITH A VOLCANO.

ARROW... *POISONED.*

DOC, HOLD ON TO ME! DON'T LET GO!

LE FAY. THAT MEANS... DON'T LET HIM TAKE US TO...

THACK

I THINK IT'S *TUESDAY*. BUT I'M NOT REALLY SURE.

NOT EVEN SURE WHAT *MONTH* IT IS ANYMORE.

ON TUESDAYS, I'D EAT MY LUNCH ON THE ROOF OF THE LIBRARY.

MY USUAL CHICKEN SANDWICH AND COTTAGE CHEESE ALWAYS SEEMED MORE EXCITING WHEN I WAS UP THERE, LOOKING OUT AT THE CITY.

RIGHT NOW I WOULD *MURDER SOMEONE'S MOTHER* FOR A CUP OF COTTAGE CHEESE.

SCRUNCH

I WOULD MURDER THEM RIGHT IN THEIR FACE.

AND THE ROOF OF THE LIBRARY? YEAH.

I MISS THAT *VIEW* MOST OF ALL.

GRUBS AND ROCK SNAILS. THAT'S ALL WE'VE GOT FOR LUNCH *AGAIN* TODAY.

ONLY FRUITS I'VE EVER FOUND IN THIS PLACE SMELL LIKE A CHEMICAL FIRE AND BURN LIKE ACID WHEN I TOUCH THEM.

AND THOSE ARE THE *GOOD* PLANTS, THAT *DON'T* TRY TO EAT YOU.

SURE, THERE'S *MEAT* TO BE HAD. LOTS OF MEAT.

THERE ARE FLYING SPIDERS AND TIGERS WITH TENTACLES AND DOGS THAT GLOW IN THE DARK AND RATS THE SIZE OF WOLVES AND WOLVES THE SIZE OF RHINOS.

BUT SO FAR, I'VE BEEN A BIT TOO BUSY NOT GETTING *KILLED* BY THOSE THINGS TO TRY AND HUNT THEM.

GRUBS AND SNAILS WILL HAVE TO BE ENOUGH.

ENOUGH TO KEEP HIM *ALIVE* FOR ANOTHER DAY.

HIS FEVER IS WORSE THAN EVER. THE POISON FROM THE ARROW IS STILL WREAKING HAVOC ON HIS BODY.

I HAVE NO IDEA HOW HE ISN'T ALREADY DEAD. AND I HAVE EVEN *LESS* OF AN IDEA ABOUT HOW TO SAVE HIM.

BIKE'S BEEN OUT OF GAS FOR *DAYS*. AS FAR AS I CAN TELL, WE'RE ON SOME SORT OF FLOATING ISLAND THAT'S PART REN FEST ON CRACK, PART POST-APOCALYPTIC GAME PRESERVE.

IN HIS FEVERISH MUMBLING, DOC SEEMS TO CALL IT *WEIRDWORLD*.

THERE'S NO WAY TO CONTACT THE OUTSIDE WORLD. NO WAY TO GET BACK THERE.

ALL I'VE GOT IS A *MAGIC WAND* I'M AFRAID TO EVEN TOUCH...

...AND A *BOOK OF SPELLS*.

THE VERY *LAST* BOOK OF SPELLS.

SINCE THE EMPIRIKUL TORCHED THE DOC'S LIBRARY, I'VE BEEN HELPING HIM REBUILD IT, RECORDING ALL THE SPELLS OF HIS THAT STILL WORK.

SURELY THERE'S *ONE* IN HERE THAT COULD SAVE HIS LIFE. BUT I'M NO MASTER OF THE MYSTIC ARTS. I'M JUST HIS GHOSTWRITER.

EVERY NIGHT I TRY TO STUMBLE THROUGH A FEW OF THESE WORDS JUST TO SEE WHAT WILL HAPPEN, BUT SO FAR ALL I'VE GOT TO SHOW FOR IT IS A BLISTERING HEADACHE.

BUT HEADACHE OR NO, IF I DON'T FIGURE SOMETHING OUT SOON, HE'S GOING TO DIE. AND THEN *I'M* GOING TO DIE.

BY THE MYSTIC MOONS OF MUNNOPOR...

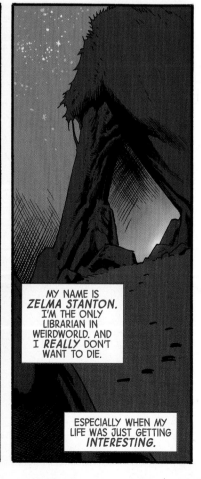

MY NAME IS *ZELMA STANTON*. I'M THE ONLY LIBRARIAN IN WEIRDWORLD. AND I *REALLY* DON'T WANT TO DIE.

ESPECIALLY WHEN MY LIFE WAS JUST GETTING *INTERESTING*.

THESE ARE *HUMAN* TRACKS. FRESH ONES.

SO AT LEAST *ONE* OF THEM IS STILL ALIVE.

BUT WHICH? THE GIRL OR THE SORCERER?

I PUT AN ARROW IN THE WIZARD, ITS POINT DIPPED IN DRAGON BILE POISON. THERE'S NO WAY HE'S STILL BREATHING.

DOESN'T MATTER WHICH OF THEM IT IS. JUST AS LONG AS THEY'VE STILL GOT THE *WAND*.

BLOODBOARS HAVE GOT THE SCENT. WON'T BE LONG NOW.

SEND WORD TO MISTRESS LE FAY. TELL HER THE *MAGMA MEN* WILL SOON BE BRINGING HER THE WAND...

...AND THE HEAD OF THE *SORCERER SUPREME*.

BLOODBOARS. THAT DOESN'T SOUND GOOD.

THEY'RE HEADING TOWARD THE CAVE. GOT TO GET AHEAD OF THEM SOMEHOW AND MOVE STRANGE BEFORE THEY...

GAAGH!

LOOKS LIKE IT WON'T BE JUST THE WIZARD'S HEAD WE'RE FETCHING FOR THE QUEEN.

YOU'LL SURE LOOK AWFUL PRETTY ON A PIKE, LITTLE DANDELION.

OH BOY.

BY THE MOONS OF MUNNOPOR...

WHAT'S THAT YOU'RE MUMBLING? YOUR PRAYERS, LITTLE FLOWER?

OR DO YOU THINK THAT YOU'RE A WIZARD, TOO?

NOT A WIZARD.

FA-SHOOOOM

BUT I DO BELIEVE IN MAGIC.

AND I KNOW...I KNOW A THING OR TWO ABOUT...

THERE'S A PRICE TO EVERYTHING A SORCERER DOES. THAT'S WHAT THE DOC WOULD SAY. NEVER REALLY UNDERSTOOD WHAT HE MEANT.

WHY DO I SUDDENLY FEEL SO...

UNTIL NOW.

HHHHEEEERRSHHH

MY FACE SMELLS LIKE REGURGITATED GRUB. WHOLE BODY FEELS LIKE IT'S ON FIRE. BUT I'M NOT *DEAD.*

IF THAT'S THE PRICE...

THERE SHE IS! AFTER HER!

...IT'S ONE I'LL *GLADLY* PAY.

DOC! NOW WOULD BE A REALLY GOOD TIME TO WAKE UP!

BUT IT'S NOT ABOUT ME.

DOC!

THERE! SHE'S IN THE CAVE!

OH, DOC. I'M SO SORRY.

I'M A LIBRARIAN FROM THE BRONX. I'M NOT UNIQUE. I'M NOTHING SPECIAL REALLY.

I'M NOT EVEN ALL THAT *WEIRD.* AND I'M CERTAINLY NO SORCERER SUPREME.

BUT IF I'M GOING DOWN...

...I'M GONNA DIE WITH A *BOOK* IN MY HAND.

BY THE VAPORS OF...

I BELIEVE IN MAGIC.

I'VE SEEN IT IN ACTION.

ZELMA! *HOLD ON!*

BUT MAGIC ISN'T FOR PEOPLE LIKE *ME.*

WHEN A NORMAL GIRL LIKE ME COMES INTO CONTACT WITH WEIRD STUFF LIKE THAT...

...IT ONLY EVER ENDS ONE WAY.

SHE SHOULD BE DEAD. *HOW* IS SHE NOT DEAD?

THE SPELL SHE SOMEHOW MANAGED TO PULL OFF, IT WAS A SPELL OF *TRANSFERENCE.*

IT SHOULD'VE KILLED HER INSTANTLY.

SHE TOOK THE POISON, THE SICKNESS OUT OF MY BODY, AND TRANSFERRED IT INTO HER OWN.

HER BODY ISN'T EQUIPPED TO FIGHT OFF A POISON LIKE THAT.

SHE DOESN'T HAVE THE MAGICAL ANTIBODIES I'VE BUILT UP OVER THE LAST SEVERAL *YEARS.* SHE DOESN'T...

MY GODS, ZELMA. WHAT HAVE YOU DONE TO YOURSELF?

WHATEVER IT WAS, IT WASN'T *ENOUGH.*

WEIRDWORLD. SHE WAS SCAVENGING FOR FOOD IN WEIRDWORLD. FOR DAYS. KEEPING US BOTH ALIVE.

SHE WAS ABSORBING THE MAGIC OF THAT PLACE IN WHATEVER SHE WAS EATING. SHE WAS PRIMING HER BODY WITHOUT EVEN KNOWING IT.

177A BLEECKER STREET, GREENWICH VILLAGE, NEW YORK. OR WHAT'S LEFT OF IT.

BANG BANG BANG CRASH

→SNARRLL←

STOP! STOP IT!!!

WHAT ARE YOU *DOING?!* YOU WERE HIRED TO EFFECT REPAIRS NOT CREATE *MORE* RUBBLE!

TWO STEPS FORWARD, ONE STEP BACK IS ALWAYS THE WAY. ROOT OUT THE *ROT.* IMPROVE THE *STOCK.* STAY OUTTA MY WAY.

YOU WERE CONTRACTED FOR FLOORS AND TILE. AND SPEAKING OF TILE, THE DOWNSTAIRS BATH IS UNACCEPTABLE.

IF YOU HAVE OUTSTANDING ISSUES, THEN PUT 'EM ON THE PUNCH LIST.

THE *PUNCH LIST* IS AS LONG AS MY ARM.

FUNNY, THAT. MINE'S ONLY GOT THE ONE THING ON IT AT THE MOMENT. STRANGE, INNIT?

NOT STRANGE AT ALL, YOU CORDLESS-TOOLED GORILLA. BUT IF YOU THINK I'M GOING TO TOLERATE IDLE--

STRANGE. BEHIND YOU.

TWITCH

STEPHEN?

JUST PULLING YOUR LEG. CAN I GET BACK TO WORK, YOUR WORSHIP?

FIVE YEARS LATER...

WHAT IS--

--IT.

HELLO, STEPHEN.

I--

STEPHEN, IT'S ME. CLEA.

I KNOW.

WE NEED TO TALK. CAN I COME IN?

YES, OF COURSE. PLEASE, WELCOME.

TEA?

YES!

HOW DOES ANYONE FIND A DAMN THING IN THIS MESS? I CAN'T BELIEVE--

STEPHEN.

STEPHEN.

CLEA, ARE YOU HERE TO HELP ME?

NOT PRECISELY. MAYBE. I'M NOT SURE.

BECAUSE I COULD REALLY USE YOU RIGHT NOW.

THAT'S WHAT I'M AFRAID OF.

WHAT IS **THAT** SUPPOSED TO MEAN?

IT MEANS THAT I'M NOT A **RESOURCE**, STEPHEN. WHATEVER POWER I STILL HAVE IS NOT YOURS TO ADD TO YOUR STOCKPILE OF MAGICAL OBJECTS. I **KNOW** YOU ARE NOT WHAT YOU ONCE WERE.

I AM **MORE** THAN MY POWER. THAT IS WHY I WAS WILLING TO GIVE IT ALL UP IN THE FIGHT FOR SURVIVAL.

WHERE WERE **YOU**?

"WHERE WERE YOU WHEN THE REST OF US WERE FIGHTING FOR OUR VERY EXISTENCE?"

"WHEN MAGIC WAS FLOWING OUT OF THIS WORLD LIKE A RIPPED ARTERY DRAINING INTO A WARM SALT OCEAN.

"WHERE WERE YOU WHEN THE **EMPIRIKUL** CAME?"

...I'M HERE NOW.

DO YOU REMEMBER, ALL THOSE YEARS AGO, WHEN WE WERE FIRST MARRIED?

OF COURSE I REMEMBER. I THOUGHT IT WOULD LAST FOREVER. AH...KETTLE.

STEPHEN, IT WAS...IT *IS* A *MYSTICAL UNION.* IT *WILL* LAST FOREVER. UNLESS...

"TWO RINGS MYSTICALLY ARE ONE. THOUGH A THOUSAND UNIVERSES SEPARATE THE TWO WEARERS, THEY CAN NEVER BE KEPT APART. WE ARE TOGETHER AT A WISH--"

THAT'S RIGHT. "AS WE SHOULD BE."

BUT IT DIDN'T WORK OUT THAT WAY.

WE BOTH HAD THINGS TO DO. DEMONS TO FIGHT. DARK DIMENSIONS TO RULE.

WHY ARE YOU HERE? WHY NOW?

BECAUSE WE ARE *STILL* BOUND AND I AM STILL *EMPOWERED.*

AND?

AND YOU NEED TO BE ABLE TO REBUILD. YOU NEED TO BE AS STRONG AS YOU CAN BE. I AM CONCERNED THAT OUR UNION IS A DRAW ON WHATEVER POWER YOU HAVE LEFT.

THAT IS *RIDICULOUS.* WHERE IS THE DAMN TEA?

IT'S NOT, STEPHEN.

WONG!

WHAT'S RIDICULOUS IS YOU IGNORING THE POSSIBILITY THAT WHAT I'M SAYING IS TRUE.

IT'S *ABSURD.* TELL YOU WHAT, WHY DON'T YOU CUT MY HAIR AND SEE IF THAT ALSO HAS AN EFFECT!

WONG!

HAVE YOU FORGOTTEN THAT I HAVE LEFT YOU BEFORE BECAUSE THE GROWING IMBALANCE IN OUR POWERS BECAME TOO MUCH TO BEAR?

YOU LEFT BECAUSE I HAD NOTHING LEFT TO TEACH YOU.

STEPHEN, *PLEASE...* THAT'S NOT WHAT HAPPENED AND YOU KNOW IT.

I AM *TRYING* TO MAKE US SOME TEA.

WONG, I NEED SOME HELP!

STEPHEN'S ROOM   WONG'S ROOM

JANGLE JANG JANG

WHO ARE *YOU?*

ZELMA. LIBRARIAN. BACK FROM TWO AMAZING WEEKS IN JAMAICA.

I MEAN, IT WAS *GLORIOUS.* I DON'T THINK I'VE EVER BEEN SO RELAXED. I *REALLY* LIKE YOUR *LEOTARD.*

ARE YOU NORMALLY LIKE THIS?

LEOTARDS? *NOT* REALLY MY THING. BUT YOU MAKE IT WORK. I MEAN--

ALL RIGHT. SHUT UP.

OH, HELLO!

HOLD STILL. THIS WON'T HURT.

ZELMA, YOU'RE BACK! HAVE A GOOD TIME?

AN *AMAZING* TIME, BUT NOW I'M BACK IN THIS @#$% HOLE AND I'M MISERABLE! WHAT DID YOU DO TO ME?!

I TRANSFERRED YOUR BLISS TO THE DEMON, BUT IT WON'T LAST.

WE NEED TO BREAK WHATEVER CONTRACT YOU SIGNED-- OR THE HOUSE, AND MAYBE ME WITH IT, IS GOING STRAIGHT TO ZANAX.

XYCORAX, AND WHAT THE HELL IS THAT?

THAT SHOULDN'T BE HERE. NOT NOW.

IT WAS OUTSIDE.

LOOKS LIKE INTERNATIONAL OVERNIGHT. AT LEAST *SOMEONE* HAS MONEY TO RUN A DECENT OPERATION. HOW NICE FOR THEM! GOD! I'M SO PISSED OFF!

NOW? YOU WANT TO DO THIS *NOW*?

NO! IT WAS ENCHANTED TO APPEAR AT THE BEST TIME OF NEED. WHEN WE COULD TALK CALMLY ABOUT DISSOLVING OUR UNION. IT SHOULDN'T...

OH...

IT'S FOR *WONG*. YOU MUST REALLY LOVE HIM.

I PUT EVERYTHING I HAD INTO IT. IT WILL DISSOLVE ANY MAGICAL CONTRACT. IT'S HERE FOR YOU AND YOUR DEMON BUILDER.

THEN LET'S USE IT.

THAT IS AN INCREDIBLY POWERFUL OBJECT BEST PRESERVED. WE CAN TRY TO SEEK ANOTHER SOLUTION.

IT'S GOING TO BE A LONG TIME BEFORE EITHER OF US CAN SUMMON THE STRENGTH FOR SOMETHING LIKE THAT AGAIN. DON'T *WASTE* IT.

HE'S COMING ROUND. IF ANYONE CARES. I SURE AS HELL DON'T.

RRRRRIIIIIIIIIPPPPP

DO WE HAVE SOME WAY TO HOLD HIM WHILE WE SORT OUT HIS BANISHMENT?

I BELIEVE SO.

THEN CAN YOU AND ZELMA ESCORT HIM DOWNSTAIRS. PLEASE.

OF COURSE.

HOW ARE YOU FEELING?

DOWNGRADED FROM PISSED TO MIFFED. I STILL THINK THERE WAS ANOTHER WAY.

I AGREE. BUT I DO THANK YOU FOR PRIORITIZING MY WELFARE.

HA!

PARDON ME?

THAT'S NOT WHAT HE DID. THE DOCTOR WAS TRYING TO PROVE SOMETHING TO THAT MAGIC CHICK. I CAN TELL.

WONG IS MORE IMPORTANT TO ME THAN *ANY* MAGICAL OBJECT.

YEAH, BUT CLEA'S KIND OF A MAGICAL OBJECT TOO, ISN'T SHE? AND NOW SHE *TRUSTS* YOU. PROBABLY THINKS YOU SEE HER AS A *PERSON* FIRST. GOOD JOB.

THINK WHAT YOU WANT. I'M GOING TO BED.

TELL ME I'M NOT WRONG, DOCTOR S! TELL ME I'M NOT WRONG!

NO.

YOU'RE NOT WRONG.

END.

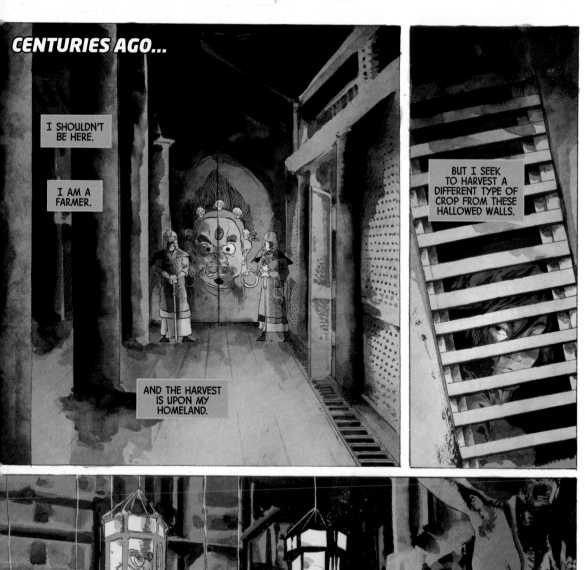

I SHOULDN'T BE HERE.

I AM A FARMER.

AND THE HARVEST IS UPON MY HOMELAND.

BUT I SEEK TO HARVEST A DIFFERENT TYPE OF CROP FROM THESE HALLOWED WALLS.

I SEEK TO HARVEST *MAGIC.*

NOW, AS I WAS SAYING. TO FIND WHAT WAS--

AH. HELLO, THERE.

GLAD YOU ALL FOLLOWED ALONG. NOW I CAN SHOW YOU MY *TRUE* ABILITIES, AND YOU WILL BOW BEFORE--

WHAK

PATHETIC.

TENDERIZE THE MEAT.

THEN TAKE HIM TO THE DUNGEON.

...THAT... ALL...YOU... GOT...?

FWOOSH

AIIGHHH!

TEALING IS MAP...

...YOU SOUGHT MMORTALITY?

...I SOUGHT FREEDOM...

YOU HAVE GREAT STRENGTH. GREAT POWER.

BUT YOU ARE A CHILD WHO BELIEVES HE IS PLAYING WITH TOYS.

YOU WILL DIE AS YOU LIVED...

...MORTAL...

...AND ALONE.

KRKLL

NO... YOU'RE JUST... A CHILD...

...I'M TOO EARLY.

...I'D SAY YOU'RE RIGHT ON TIME...

VMMMM

HOW OLD *ARE* YOU?

OLD ENOUGH TO KNOW A *FRIEND* WHEN I SEE ONE. NOW, LET'S CONTINUE THIS CONVERSATION IN A LESS--

HAVE YOU... HAVE YOU *USED* THIS MAP?

NO. BUT PERHAPS WE COULD DO SO *TOGETHER*, FRIEND. NOW, AS I WAS SAYING...

THERE'S... THERE'S NO TIME...

WHAT... WHAT ARE YOU DOING? THIS MAGIC, IT'S DARK, TWISTED-- WHAT POWERS HAVE YOU MEDDLED WITH, OLD MAN?

ANY AND ALL I COULD GET MY HANDS ON, MY BOY. AS YOU CAN SEE...

...THERE IS MUCH WORK TO BE DONE.

MY NAME IS MERLIN. AND I NEED YOUR HELP.

CONTINUED IN **DOCTOR STRANGE AND THE SORCERERS SUPREME**.

STRANGE TALES:
YAO, THE NOT-QUITE-ANCIENT ONE

DOCTOR
STRANGE

ANNUAL #1 HIP-HOP VARIANT BY **THEOTIS JONES**